46 to ONE

A Journal

By

_____

ADK 46R # _____

Graphics North
Jay, New York, USA

Graphics North, Jay, NY 12941

© 2004, 2006, 2009 by Nadine McLaughlin. All rights reserved.
Published 2004, Second Printing 2006, Third Printing 2009
Printed in the United States of America
Printed in China

Library of Congress Control Number: 2004115119

ISBN # 0-9643452-5-0

**Front Cover Photo: Carl Heilman
Back Cover Photos: Marcia Hanson
Book Design and Illustrations: Nadine McLaughlin**

Published by Graphics North
PO Box 218, Jay, NY 12941, USA

The Day Off

This day was mine,
to do with as I pleased,
to spend or squander
— or invest —
in any way
that seemed the best
for me.

And so, I chose
to use the hours
of my precious day—
to grow myself
in joyful ways
that no one else
may understand...
but me.

Today, I climbed
above my daily life
and brought back down
to earth with me
a mountain lake,
a summit high,
a portion of the sun-lit sky
to cherish
in my memory's eye:

A golden treasure,
saved today
for future,
less-inspiring days
when "rules" and "shoulds"
again conspire
to keep my soul
from being free.

Nadine McLaughlin

to ADK 46R #1582

Contents

Journal pages are not numbered. Each of the 46 High Peaks is in sequence by the following alphabetical order:

- **A.** Algonquin Peak
  Allen Mtn.
  Armstrong Mtn.
- **B.** Basin Mtn.
  Big Slide Mtn.
  Blake Peak
- **C.** Cascade Mtn.
  Cliff Mtn.
  Couchsachraga Peak
- **D.** Dial Mtn.
  Dix Mtn.
- **E.** East Dix
  Esther Mtn.
- **G.** Giant Mt.
  Gothics
  Gray Peak
- **H.** Hough Peak
- **I.** Iroquois Peak
- **L.** Lower Wolf Jaw Mtn.
- **M.** Macomb Mtn.
  Mt. Colden
  Mt. Colvin
  Mt. Donaldson
  Mt. Emmons
  Mt. Haystack

    Mt. Marcy
    Mt. Marshall
    Mt. Redfield
    Mt. Skylight
- **N.** Nipple Top
  Nye Mtn.
- **P.** Panther Peak
  Phelps Mtn.
  Porter Mtn.
- **R.** Rocky Ridge Peak
- **S.** Saddleback Mtn.
  Santanoni Peak
  Sawteeth
  Seward Mtn.
  Seymour Mtn.
  South Dix
  Street Mtn.
- **T.** Table Top Mtn.
- **U.** Upper Wolf Jaw Mtn.
- **W.** Whiteface Mtn.
  Wright Peak

(See page following Wright Peak's entry for McNaughton Mtn. *also 4000 ft., but not designated as one of the official 46 High Peaks.)*

Preface

Why (and when) I decided to climb all 46 of the highest Adirondack mountains:

_____
_____
_____
_____
_____
_____
_____

The first mountain I climbed was: _____ Date: _____

My age when I started the climbs: _____

Physical condition then: _____ Weight: _____

The last mountain I climbed was: _____

Date of the climb: _____ My age when I finished the last climb: _____

Physical condition then: _____ Weight: _____

What climbing these mountains has meant to me:

_____
_____

(continued on next page)

The 46 High Peaks in Order of Their Height Above Sea Level

Mt. Marcy . . . . .5344 ft.	Rocky Ridge Peak . . . . .4420 ft.	Mt. Colvin . . . . .4057 ft.
Algonquin Peak . . . . .5114 ft.	Macomb Mtn. . . . . .4405 ft.	Mt. Emmons . . . . .4040 ft.
Mt. Haystack . . . . .4960 ft.	Armstrong Mtn. . . . . .4400 ft.	Dial Mtn. . . . . .4020 ft.
Mt. Skylight . . . . .4926 ft.	Hough Peak . . . . .4400 ft.	East Dix . . . . .4012 ft.
Whiteface Mtn. . . . . .4867 ft.	Seward Mtn. . . . . .4361 ft.	*Blake Peak . . . . .3960 ft.
Dix Mtn. . . . . .4857 ft.	Mt. Marshall . . . . .4360 ft.	*Cliff Mtn. . . . . .3960 ft.
Gray Peak . . . . .4840 ft.	Allen Mtn. . . . . .4340 ft.	*Nye Mtn. . . . . .3895 ft.
Iroquois Peak . . . . .4840 ft.	Big Slide Mtn. . . . . .4240 ft.	*Couchsachraga Peak . . . . . . .3820 ft
Basin Mtn. . . . . .4827 ft.	Esther Mtn. . . . . .4240 ft.	
Gothics . . . . .4736 ft.	Upper Wolf Jaw Mtn. . . . . . . .4185 ft.	
Mt. Colden . . . . 4714 ft.	Lower Wolf Jaw Mtn. . . . . . . .4175 ft.	
Giant Mt. . . . . .4627 ft.	Street Mtn. . . . . .4166 ft.	
Nipple Top . . . . .4620 ft.	Phelps Mtn. . . . . 4161 ft.	
Santanoni Peak . . . . .4607 ft.	Mt. Donaldson . . . . .4140 ft.	
Mt. Redfield . . . . .4606 ft.	Seymour Mtn. . . . . .4120 ft.	
Wright Peak . . . . .4580 ft.	Sawteeth . . . . .4100 ft.	
Saddleback Mtn. . . . . .4515 ft.	Cascade Mtn. . . . . .4098 ft.	
Panther Peak . . . . .4442 ft.	South Dix . . . . .4060 ft.	
Table Top Mtn. . . . . .4427 ft.	Porter Mtn. . . . . .4059 ft.	

* Early surveys of these last four mountains identified them as being at least 4000 ft. high. Although more recent surveys lowered their heights, they remain a part of the group of major mountains qualifying climbers for membership in the Adirondack 46Rs.

One other Adirondack mountain (MacNaughton) is also 4000 ft. high, but it is not officially designated as one of the 46 High Peaks and not required for membership in the Adirondack 46Rs. (See page at the back following Wright Peak entry for this optional mountain climb.)

The Order of My Climbs of the 46 High Peaks

Mountain   Date   Mountain   Date

1. _____ 11. _____

2. _____ 12. _____

3. _____ 13. _____

4. _____ 14. _____

5. _____ 15. _____

6. _____ 16. _____

7. _____ 17. _____

8. _____ 18. _____

9. _____ 19. _____

10. _____ 20. _____

Mountain	Date	Mountain	Date
21.		34.	
22.		35.	
23.		36.	
24.		37.	
25.		38.	
26.		39.	
27.		40.	
28.		41.	
29.		42.	
30.		43.	
31.		44.	
32.		45.	
33.		46.	

The hardest climb: _____ The easiest: _____

The most fun: _____ The best view: _____

46
to ONE

A Journal

Algonquin Peak ~ 5114 ft.

Date of Climb: _____

Weather Conditions: _____
_____

Time of Departure: _____ A.M./P.M.

From: _____ Trailhead

Returned at: _____ A.M./P.M.

Companions:
_____
_____
_____
_____

Other Summits reached today:
_____
_____

Highlight of the climb: _____
_____
_____
_____
_____

Allen Mtn. ~ 4340 ft.

Date of Climb: _____

Weather Conditions: _____
_____

Time of Departure: _____ A.M./P.M.

From: _____ Trailhead

Returned at: _____ A.M./P.M.

Companions:
_____
_____
_____
_____

Other Summits reached today:
_____
_____

Highlight of the climb:
_____
_____
_____
_____

Armstrong Mtn. ~ 4400 ft.

Date of Climb: _____

Weather Conditions: _____
_____

Time of Departure: _____ A.M./P.M.

From: _____ Trailhead

Returned at: _____ A.M./P.M.

Companions:
_____
_____
_____
_____

Other Summits reached today:
_____
_____

Highlight of the climb: _____
_____
_____
_____

Basin Mtn. ~ 4827 ft.

Date of Climb:

Weather Conditions:

Time of Departure: _____ A.M./P.M.

From: _____ Trailhead

Returned at: _____ A.M./P.M.

Companions:

Other Summits reached today:

Highlight of the climb:

Big Slide Mtn. ~ 4240 ft.

Date of Climb:

Weather Conditions:

Time of Departure: _____ A.M./P.M.

From: _____ Trailhead

Returned at: _____ A.M./P.M.

Companions:

Other Summits reached today:

Highlight of the climb:

Blake Peak ~ 3960 ft.

Date of Climb:

Weather Conditions:

Time of Departure: _____ A.M./P.M.

From: _____ Trailhead

Returned at: _____ A.M./P.M.

Companions:

Other Summits reached today:

Highlight of the climb:

Cascade Mtn. ~ 4098 ft.

Date of Climb: _____

Weather Conditions: _____
_____

Time of Departure: _____ A.M./P.M.

From: _____ Trailhead

Returned at: _____ A.M./P.M.

Companions:
_____
_____
_____
_____

Other Summits reached today:
_____
_____

Highlight of the climb: _____
_____
_____
_____

Cliff Mtn. ~ 3960 ft.

Date of Climb: _____

Weather Conditions: _____
_____

Time of Departure: _____ A.M./P.M.

From: _____ Trailhead

Returned at: _____ A.M./P.M.

Companions:
_____
_____
_____
_____

Other Summits reached today:
_____
_____

Highlight of the climb: _____
_____
_____
_____

Couchsachraga Peak ~ 3820 ft.

Date of Climb: _____

Weather Conditions: _____
_____

Time of Departure: _____ A.M./P.M.

From: _____ Trailhead

Returned at: _____ A.M./P.M.

Companions:
_____
_____
_____
_____

Other Summits reached today:
_____
_____

Highlight of the climb: _____
_____
_____
_____

Dial Mtn. ~ 4020 ft.

Date of Climb: _____

Weather Conditions: _____
_____

Time of Departure: _____ A.M./P.M.

From: _____ Trailhead

Returned at: _____ A.M./P.M.

Companions:
_____
_____
_____
_____

Other Summits reached today:
_____
_____

Highlight of the climb: _____
_____
_____
_____

Dix Mtn. ~ 4857 ft.

Date of Climb: _____

Weather Conditions: _____
_____
_____

Time of Departure: _____ A.M./P.M.

From: _____ Trailhead

Returned at: _____ A.M./P.M.

Companions:
_____
_____
_____
_____

Other Summits reached today:
_____
_____
_____

Highlight of the climb: _____
_____
_____
_____
_____

East Dix ~ 4012 ft.

Date of Climb: _____

Weather Conditions: _____
_____

Time of Departure: _____ A.M./P.M.

From: _____ Trailhead

Returned at: _____ A.M./P.M.

Companions:
_____
_____
_____
_____

Other Summits reached today:
_____

Highlight of the climb: _____
_____
_____
_____
_____

Esther Mtn. ~ 4240 ft.

Date of Climb: _____

Weather Conditions: _____
_____

Time of Departure: _____ A.M./P.M.

From: _____ Trailhead

Returned at: _____ A.M./P.M.

Companions:
_____
_____
_____
_____

Other Summits reached today:
_____
_____

Highlight of the climb: _____
_____
_____

Giant Mtn. ~ 4627 ft.

Date of Climb: _____

Weather Conditions: _____
_____

Time of Departure: _____ A.M./P.M.

From: _____ Trailhead

Returned at: _____ A.M./P.M.

Companions:
_____
_____
_____
_____

Other Summits reached today:
_____
_____

Highlight of the climb: _____
_____
_____
_____

Gothics ~ 4736 ft.

Date of Climb: _____

Weather Conditions: _____
_____

Time of Departure: _____ A.M./P.M.

From: _____ Trailhead

Returned at: _____ A.M./P.M.

Companions:
_____
_____
_____
_____

Other Summits reached today:
_____
_____

Highlight of the climb: _____
_____
_____
_____

Gray Peak ~ 4840 ft.

Date of Climb: _____

Weather Conditions: _____
_____

Time of Departure: _____ A.M./P.M.

From: _____ Trailhead

Returned at: _____ A.M./P.M.

Companions:
_____
_____
_____
_____

Other Summits reached today:
_____
_____

Highlight of the climb: _____
_____
_____
_____
_____

Hough Peak ~ 4400 ft.

Date of Climb: _____

Weather Conditions: _____
_____

Time of Departure: _____ A.M./P.M.

From: _____ Trailhead

Returned at: _____ A.M./P.M.

Companions:
_____
_____
_____
_____
_____

Other Summits reached today:
_____
_____

Highlight of the climb: _____
_____
_____
_____

Iroquois Peak ~ 4840 ft.

Date of Climb: _____

Weather Conditions: _____
_____

Time of Departure: _____ A.M./P.M.

From: _____ Trailhead

Returned at: _____ A.M./P.M.

Companions:
_____
_____
_____
_____

Other Summits reached today:
_____
_____

Highlight of the climb: _____
_____
_____
_____

Lower Wolf Jaw Mtn. ~ 4175 ft.

Date of Climb: _____

Weather Conditions: _____
_____

Time of Departure: _____ A.M./P.M.

From: _____ Trailhead

Returned at: _____ A.M./P.M.

Companions:
_____
_____
_____
_____

Other Summits reached today:
_____
_____

Highlight of the climb: _____
_____
_____
_____

Macomb Mtn. ~ 4405 ft.

Date of Climb:

Weather Conditions:

Time of Departure: _____ A.M./P.M.

From: _____ Trailhead

Returned at: _____ A.M./P.M.

Companions:

Other Summits reached today:

Highlight of the climb:

Mt. Colden ~ 4714 ft.

Date of Climb: _____

Weather Conditions: _____

Time of Departure: _____ A.M./P.M.

From: _____ Trailhead

Returned at: _____ A.M./P.M.

Companions:
_____
_____
_____
_____

Other Summits reached today:
_____
_____

Highlight of the climb:
_____
_____
_____

Mt. Colvin ~ 4057 ft.

Date of Climb: _____

Weather Conditions: _____
_____

Time of Departure: _____ A.M./P.M.

From: _____ Trailhead

Returned at: _____ A.M./P.M.

Companions:
_____
_____
_____
_____

Other Summits reached today:
_____
_____

Highlight of the climb: _____
_____
_____
_____

Mt. Donaldson ~ 4140 ft.

Date of Climb: _____

Weather Conditions: _____
_____

Time of Departure: _____ A.M./P.M.

From: _____ Trailhead

Returned at: _____ A.M./P.M.

Companions:
_____
_____
_____
_____
_____

Other Summits reached today:
_____
_____

Highlight of the climb: _____
_____
_____
_____
_____

Mt. Emmons ~ 4040 ft.

Date of Climb: _____

Weather Conditions: _____
_____

Time of Departure: _____ A.M./P.M.

From: _____ Trailhead

Returned at: _____ A.M./P.M.

Companions:
_____
_____
_____
_____

Other Summits reached today:
_____
_____

Highlight of the climb: _____
_____
_____
_____
_____

Mt. Haystack ~ 4960 ft.

Date of Climb: _____

Weather Conditions: _____
_____

Time of Departure: _____ A.M./P.M.

From: _____ Trailhead

Returned at: _____ A.M./P.M.

Companions:
_____
_____
_____
_____

Other Summits reached today:
_____
_____

Highlight of the climb:
_____
_____
_____

Mt. Marcy ~ 5344 ft.

Date of Climb: _____

Weather Conditions: _____
_____

Time of Departure: _____ A.M./P.M.

From: _____ Trailhead

Returned at: _____ A.M./P.M.

Companions:
_____
_____
_____
_____

Other Summits reached today:
_____
_____

Highlight of the climb: _____
_____
_____
_____

Mt. Marshall ~ 4360 ft.

Date of Climb: _____

Weather Conditions: _____
_____

Time of Departure: _____ A.M./P.M.
From: _____ Trailhead
Returned at: _____ A.M./P.M.
Companions:
_____
_____
_____
_____

Other Summits reached today:
_____
_____

Highlight of the climb:
_____
_____
_____
_____

Mt. Redfield ~ 4606 ft.

Date of Climb: _____

Weather Conditions: _____
_____

Time of Departure: _____ A.M./P.M.
From: _____ Trailhead
Returned at: _____ A.M./P.M.
Companions: _____
_____
_____
_____
_____

Other Summits reached today: _____
_____

Highlight of the climb: _____
_____
_____
_____
_____

Mt. Skylight ~ 4926 ft.

Date of Climb: _____

Weather Conditions: _____
_____

Time of Departure: _____ A.M./P.M.

From: _____ Trailhead

Returned at: _____ A.M./P.M.

Companions:
_____
_____
_____
_____

Other Summits reached today:
_____
_____

Highlight of the climb:
_____
_____
_____

Nipple Top ~ 4620 ft.

Date of Climb: _____

Weather Conditions: _____
_____

Time of Departure: _____ A.M./P.M.

From: _____ Trailhead

Returned at: _____ A.M./P.M.

Companions:
_____
_____
_____
_____
_____

Other Summits reached today:
_____
_____

Highlight of the climb: _____
_____
_____
_____
_____

Nye Mtn. ~ 3895 ft.

Date of Climb: _____

Weather Conditions: _____
_____

Time of Departure: _____ A.M./P.M.

From: _____ Trailhead

Returned at: _____ A.M./P.M.

Companions:
_____
_____
_____
_____

Other Summits reached today:
_____
_____

Highlight of the climb: _____
_____
_____
_____

Panther Peak ~ 4442 ft.

Date of Climb: _____

Weather Conditions: _____
_____

Time of Departure: _____ A.M./P.M.

From: _____ Trailhead

Returned at: _____ A.M./P.M.

Companions:
_____
_____
_____
_____

Other Summits reached today:
_____
_____

Highlight of the climb: _____
_____
_____
_____
_____

Phelps Mtn. ~ 4161 ft.

Date of Climb: _____

Weather Conditions: _____
_____

Time of Departure: _____ A.M./P.M.

From: _____ Trailhead

Returned at: _____ A.M./P.M.

Companions:
_____
_____
_____
_____
_____

Other Summits reached today:
_____
_____

Highlight of the climb: _____
_____
_____
_____

Porter Mtn. ~ 4059 ft.

Date of Climb: _____

Weather Conditions: _____
_____

Time of Departure: _____ A.M./P.M.

From: _____ Trailhead

Returned at: _____ A.M./P.M.

Companions:
_____
_____
_____
_____

Other Summits reached today:
_____
_____

Highlight of the climb: _____
_____
_____
_____

Rocky Peak Ridge ~ 4420 ft.

Date of Climb: _____

Weather Conditions: _____
_____

Time of Departure: _____ A.M./P.M.

From: _____ Trailhead

Returned at: _____ A.M./P.M.

Companions:
_____
_____
_____
_____

Other Summits reached today:
_____
_____

Highlight of the climb: _____
_____
_____
_____
_____

Saddleback Mtn. ~ 4515 ft.

Date of Climb: _____

Weather Conditions: _____
_____

Time of Departure: _____ A.M./P.M.

From: _____ Trailhead

Returned at: _____ A.M./P.M.

Companions:
_____
_____
_____
_____

Other Summits reached today:
_____
_____

Highlight of the climb: _____
_____
_____
_____

Santanoni Peak ~ 4607 ft.

Date of Climb: _____

Weather Conditions:
_____

Time of Departure: _____ A.M./P.M.
From: _____ Trailhead
Returned at: _____ A.M./P.M.
Companions:
_____
_____
_____
_____
_____

Other Summits reached today:
_____
_____
_____

Highlight of the climb: _____
_____
_____
_____

Sawteeth ~ 4100 ft.

Date of Climb: _____

Weather Conditions: _____

_____

Time of Departure: _____ A.M./P.M.

From: _____ Trailhead

Returned at: _____ A.M./P.M.

Companions:

_____

_____

_____

_____

Other Summits reached today:

_____

_____

Highlight of the climb: _____

_____

_____

_____

_____

Seward Mtn. ~ 4361 ft.

Date of Climb: _____

Weather Conditions: _____
_____

Time of Departure: _____ A.M./P.M.

From: _____ Trailhead

Returned at: _____ A.M./P.M.

Companions:
_____
_____
_____
_____

Other Summits reached today:
_____
_____

Highlight of the climb: _____
_____
_____
_____
_____

Seymour Mtn. ~ 4120 ft.

Date of Climb: _____

Weather Conditions: _____
_____

Time of Departure: _____ A.M./P.M.

From: _____ Trailhead

Returned at: _____ A.M./P.M.

Companions:
_____
_____
_____
_____

Other Summits reached today:
_____
_____

Highlight of the climb: _____
_____
_____
_____

South Dix ~ 4060 ft.

Date of Climb: _____

Weather Conditions: _____
_____

Time of Departure: _____ A.M./P.M.

From: _____ Trailhead

Returned at: _____ A.M./P.M.

Companions:
_____
_____
_____
_____

Other Summits reached today:
_____
_____

Highlight of the climb: _____
_____
_____
_____
_____

Street Mtn. ~ 4166 ft.

Date of Climb: _____

Weather Conditions: _____
_____

Time of Departure: _____ A.M./P.M.

From: _____ Trailhead

Returned at: _____ A.M./P.M.

Companions:
_____
_____
_____
_____

Other Summits reached today:
_____
_____

Highlight of the climb: _____
_____
_____
_____

Table Top Mtn. ~ 4427 ft.

Date of Climb: _____

Weather Conditions: _____
_____

Time of Departure: _____ A.M./P.M.

From: _____ Trailhead

Returned at: _____ A.M./P.M.

Companions:
_____
_____
_____
_____

Other Summits reached today:
_____
_____

Highlight of the climb: _____
_____
_____
_____

Upper Wolf Jaw Mtn. ~ 4185 ft.

Date of Climb:

Weather Conditions:

Time of Departure: _____ A.M./P.M.

From: _____ Trailhead

Returned at: _____ A.M./P.M.

Companions:

Other Summits reached today:

Highlight of the climb:

Whiteface Mtn. ~ 4867 ft.

Date of Climb:

Weather Conditions:

Time of Departure: _____ A.M./P.M.

From: _____ Trailhead

Returned at: _____ A.M./P.M.

Companions:

Other Summits reached today:

Highlight of the climb:

Wright Peak ~ 4580 ft.

Date of Climb: _____

Weather Conditions: _____
_____

Time of Departure: _____ A.M./P.M.

From: _____ Trailhead

Returned at: _____ A.M./P.M.

Companions:
_____
_____
_____
_____

Other Summits reached today:
_____
_____

Highlight of the climb: _____
_____
_____
_____

McNaughton (the forgotten) Mtn.

Though early mappers neglected to designate this mountain as one of the 46 Adirondack High Peaks, more recent surveys have identified it as being 4,000' also. Climbing it is not a requirement to become an official 46R, yet many enjoy adding it to their list of summits attained.

I climbed McNaughton on: _____ The weather was: _____

Companions were: _____

Comments: _____

_____

_____

_____

MISCELLANEOUS NOTES ⟶